W9-AZK-982

Brain Breaks
for the Classroom

Quick and Easy Breathing and Movement Activities That Help Students Reenergize, Refocus, and Boost Brain Power—Any Time of the Day!

MICHELLE GAY, CMA

New York • Toronto • London • Auckland • Sydney
Mexico City • New Delhi • Hong Kong • Buenos Aires

Teaching *Resources*

Dedication

To my family, Bob, Riley, and Zelda—
my heart in three pieces.

Acknowledgments

Thanks to the following individuals and institutions for their support: Maria Chang for seeing the good in my work and bringing me in on this project; my editor, Sarah Longhi, who guided me every step of the way; my dear friends and colleagues, Fern Love, Amy Matthews, and Aynsley Vandenbrouke, for their laughter, patience, and sound advice; the faculty of the Laban Institute for Movement Studies, Yearlong Program, 2002, without whom I would still be looking for the words to describe what I see and do; Bonnie Bainbridge Cohen and The School for Body-Mind Centering® for their inspiration; the City & Country School, for lending their premises for photographs and for giving me a treasured place on the faculty; my fellow peaceful warriors and willing guinea pigs, Donna Green and Diane Bank, and the Society for Martial Arts Instruction—our movement laboratory; and to all of my students, young and old, who show up ready to play and learn.

> **Safety Warning!** Before using the activities in this book with students, be sure to check students' health records and/or consult with parents directly to make sure that students have no physical conditions that would make participating in these activities unsafe for them. If necessary, seek advice from the school nurse or another licensed medical professional.

Editor: Sarah Longhi
Content editor: Nicole Iorio
Design and photography by Maria Lilja and Rondell Romiel
ISBN-13 978-0-545-07474-2
ISBN-10 0-545-07474-6

1 2 3 4 5 6 7 8 9 10   40   15 14 13 12 11 10 09

Contents

Introduction

Take a deep breath. Let your whole body lengthen as you inhale and then lengthen even more as you exhale, as though your head is a balloon floating upward and your spine is the string trailing below. If you feel that you might float away altogether, stamp your feet to bring yourself back to the earth.

Teach children to use their breath and you'll teach them to pay attention to themselves, bringing awareness to their bodies on the inside and outside. It's a short step from there to students' awareness of themselves in relation to others—especially their classmates and teachers. You might say that the class that breathes together or "shares the air" is a group united in a most fundamental and potent place—the beginning.

How to Use This Book

Children seem to have an endless source of energy with which to tackle the day. They run rather than walk, jump rather than step over, and drop down rather than sit. The movement activities in *Brain Breaks for the Classroom* are designed to help you make the most of your students' energy, re-energizing and refocusing your class throughout the day.

Each activity pairs simple step-by-step directions (Action) with an imaginative prompt to enhance students' movement experience (Expression). Variations and tips are provided to offer easier modifications and more rigorous challenges. You may also want to hang the included poster in an area where individual students may follow one of the five activities listed to take a brain break independently. These options allow you to appeal to the different learning styles and physical needs of your students.

The activities also take into account the practical constraints of your busy schedule. You can choose just one brain break for students to do during a short transition or you can put together a series of exercises for a longer break. The exercises can be done any time throughout the day to foster individual and group focus.

Breaks for Body and Mind

How do we ensure that brain breaks are not only easy for students to follow, but fully engage them mentally and physically? Each brain break includes suggestions that are imaginative, playful, and physically challenging, to help keep students' body and mind working in unison. Often students come up with their own images and innovations for the exercises, and you'll find that incorporating their suggestions is a great way to motivate students. It can also deepen the sense of community in the classroom.

To begin an activity, follow the Action steps in sequence. You might find it best to read the steps aloud to your students. Alternately, you can make copies of the steps for each student to read along with you, or scan the steps and project them onto the board. However you share the directions, consider having one student practice the exercise ahead of time and demonstrate it for the class. As they repeat the activity, guide students to respond to the imagery.

All of the exercises are designed to develop the natural bond between mind and body. They differ, however, in that some activities are meant for individual focus while others are more interactive. On page 6, you'll find activity symbols that indicate the two types of focus.

What the Experts Say

I hear and I forget. I read and I understand. I do and I remember.
— Chinese Proverb

Our amazing anatomy shows us why taking brain breaks is so important for daily life in the classroom: Our nerves and blood vessels always travel together in bundles. Imagine that—the brain and heart hold and support one another from head to toe! This poetic example points out the close relationship that the nervous system shares with the cardiovascular system. The wiring is there—we just have to connect it. And brain break activities do exactly that.

The parents of children I teach often report academic and behavioral improvement, as well as boosts in their children's self-esteem. In fact, there is scientific support linking exercise and movement to improved learning.

- John Ratey, a professor of psychiatry at Harvard Medical School and the author of *Spark: The Evolutionary New Science of Exercise and the Brain* (2008), asserts that "physical activity sparks biological changes that encourage brain cells to bind to one another. . . exercise provides an unparalleled stimulus, creating an environment in which the brain is ready, willing and able to learn." (p. 10)

- Carla Hannaford, neurophysiologist, educator, and author of *Smart Moves: Why Learning Is Not All in Your Head* (1995), shows how the brain learns through specific movements that challenge the body's timing, balance, and coordination, and stimulate the senses of seeing, hearing, and touch.

- In her groundbreaking book, *Sensing, Feeling and Action*, Bonnie Bainbridge Cohen, a movement educator and the founder of The School for Body-Mind Centering®, highlights the importance of the sequence of motor development from birth to standing (basic neurological patterning). She explains how using these patterns with students opens new neurological pathways and expands "the possibilities for expression and understanding." (p. 103)

Traditional developmental patterns are:

 movement initiated by the head or spine, as in rolling (spinal)

 movement focused in the upper or lower body, as in jumping or playing leapfrog (homologous)

 movement focused in the same side of the body—right arm and right leg, as in galloping (homolateral)

 movements that cross the midline of the body, coordinating opposite sides, as in crawling, walking, and running (contralateral)

- In *The Brain That Changes Itself*, Norman Droidge, M.D., cites experiments that demonstrate lasting changes in patients who performed specific movement tasks that required their full attention to accomplish. Droidge argues that the brain adapts most effectively when paying attention to the body's intended action. It is not enough to move; we must move thoughtfully!

As you and your class try out the activities in this book and innovate on them, remind your students to pay attention to their experiences—how can they make that movement more vigorous? What is happening to their breathing and heart rate? How can they improve their balance in that position? Each time students take a brain break, help them to realize that this is an opportunity to build new connections in their brains, strengthen their hearts, sharpen their ability to tap their five senses, and focus in on tasks.

Two Types of Focus

 Activities that help students prepare for individual study, focus on test taking, and redirect excess energy are marked as **inner focus.**

 Exercises that stimulate lagging attention, low energy, and can be used to prepare students for group activities are marked as **interactive focus.**

In time, your students will develop an awareness of their energy levels and be equipped with a variety of movement strategies to help them make good choices for self-regulation.

Competition and Cooperation

Both boys and girls love to feel their physical power and relish their accomplishments as they improve with each exercise. One way to support children, especially boys, who thrive on higher-intensity movement, is to add a structured competitive element (Pollack, 1998). At the same time, it's important to cultivate a cooperative atmosphere infused with creativity for students who learn best in a supportive, interpersonal environment.

As you guide students through the brain-break activities, you can balance these goals by leading students in a cooperative competition that encourages them to focus on personal achievement. You might emphasize, "How fast can I be?" or "Can I be better balanced than I was last week?" instead of "Who can be the fastest one of all?" This adds the spice of competition without spoiling it for students less athletically adept or competitive. If you enjoy leading the movements, you may also want to challenge the class to work as a team to "beat" you. For example, ask children to try to outlast your exhalation during a breathing exercise or ask, "Can you be as still as I am?" Ending an exercise in this way focuses all eyes on you, helping you transition the class to the next activity. You might also challenge students to be as slow and careful as they can during an exercise, so that the air becomes thick with concentration. This is a great way to use enthusiasm to regain control!

A Final Thought

Sometimes when I get up in the morning, I feel very peculiar. I feel like I've just got to bite a cat! I feel like if I don't bite a cat before sundown, I'll go crazy! But then I just take a deep breath and forget about it. That's what is known as real maturity.
—Snoopy, in *Peanuts*

I am inspired to finish this introduction the same way that it began, with a breath— a deep breath, a paying-attention breath. It really is the best way to begin and end any activity. It requires no special equipment, space, or coordination, and it has the unique power to both relax and invigorate us. The added benefit is that it provides a pause in which to think before doing or saying anything more.

References

Bainbridge Cohen, B. (2008). *Sensing, feeling and action*. Northampton, MA: Contact Editions.

Ratey, J. (2008). *Spark: The revolutionary new science of exercise and the brain*. New York: Little, Brown and Company.

Droidge, N. (2007). *The brain that changes itself*. New York: Penguin Books.

Hannaford, C. (1995). *Smart moves: Why learning is not all in your head*. Arlington, VA: Great Ocean Publishers.

Pollack, W. (1998). *Real boys: Rescuing our sons from the myths of boyhood*. New York: Henry Holt and Company.

Four Brain-Break Essentials

1 Get Grounded

Being grounded is a result of good balance, with our weight transferred through our center of gravity to the floor. Students who are not well grounded may have trouble sitting or standing still, communicating ideas, or listening. While all brain breaks begin in a grounded position, those listed here emphasize the skill.

Equilateral Triangle

Grounding Activities
- Standing Bow (page 12)
- X's and O's (page 14)
- Skateboarding (page 23)
- On the Run (page 26)
- Equilateral Triangle (page 28)
- Isosceles Triangle (page 29)
- Right Triangle (page 30)
- Belly Breathing (page 38)
- Swinging Samurai (page 42)

2 Raise Self-Space Awareness

Children with a good sense of self-space make smart choices about how close to be in relation to people and objects in the room. A child's sense of self-space is usually strongest in front and weaker on the sides and back. With the brain breaks listed here, students develop a better sense of their personal space.

Self-Space Activities
- Focus Ball (page 10)
- Tiger and Butterfly (page 15)
- Elasta-Kid (page 18)
- 3-D Breathing (page 39)
- Stealth Walk (page 45)

3 Practice Self-Control

Exercises that emphasize timing help students practice self-control and learn the importance of timing and tempo in exercise. All brain breaks can be modified using different timing elements, but those listed here are particularly valuable for self-control.

Self-Control Activities
- Name Toss (page 17)
- Karate Kicks (page 25)
- Invisible Kids (page 40)

4 Build Readiness to Participate

Energy and attention levels vary from student to student throughout the day, making group cohesion a challenge. Brain breaks can be used to respond to the energy levels of both individual students and the whole class. Try assigning a high-energy break to specific children and then follow it with something low-level, like a breathing exercise, to stimulate or release energy and then refocus it.

Karate Kicks

High-Energy Activities
- Name Toss (page 17)
- Cross Body Roll (page 22)
- Karate Kicks (page 25)
- On the Run (page 26)
- Iron Caterpillar (page 27)
- Bucking Bronco (page 32)
- Swinging Samurai (page 42)
- Crab Walk (page 47)

Moderate Energy Activities
- X's and O's (page 14)
- Elasta-Kid (page 18)
- The Sphinx (page 20)
- Skateboarding (page 23)
- Rolling Triangles (page 31)

Low-Energy Activities
- Head to Toe (page 9)
- Brain Wave (page 13)
- Smart Feet Sitting (page 33)
- Wriggling (page 34)
- Shake It Off (page 36)
- Belly Breathing (page 38)
- Fuzz Busters (page 41)
- Stealth Walk (page 45)

Three Rules of Good Posture

This is my "depressed stance." When you're depressed, it makes a lot of difference how you stand. The worst thing you can do is straighten up and hold your head high because then you'll start to feel better. If you're going to get any joy out of being depressed, you've got to stand like this.

—Charlie Brown, in *Peanuts*

Are your students alert and responsive? Or are they slouched over their desks? Are they leaning on an elbow or a wall? In schools, students were once required to hold themselves with a straight spine, shoulders back, and eyes front—a posture which promotes rigidity rather than alertness. You don't need such a strict formula to help your students develop good posture. Ideal posture is dynamic, self-regulating, and can take the form of varied positions that let the body and mind refresh and refocus. To help students support themselves at school, follow these simple rules:

1 Head on Top
Look for postures in which the head is clearly supported by the spine. When a child's head is held off-center, the muscles of the neck, shoulders, and upper back must work against gravity to hold it up. This gets tiring very quickly. To promote head-up posture, see Share the Air (page 16) and Floating Heads (page 19).

2 Good Base of Support
When standing, the feet are placed hip-width apart with toes facing forward and the weight evenly distributed. When sitting in chairs, both feet touch flat to the floor. When sitting on the floor, hips rest above the thighs. See Equilateral Triangle (page 28), Isosceles Triangle (page 29), and Right Triangle (page 30).

3 Curvy Spines
All four curves of the spine are present while standing and sitting. See Wriggling (page 34), Fuzz Busters (see page 41)

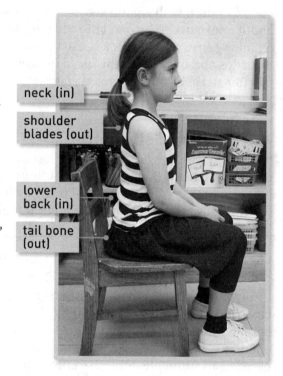

neck (in)

shoulder blades (out)

lower back (in)

tail bone (out)

Props can be used to help students fit better at their desks. Yoga blocks work well under feet, or rolled blankets to raise the seat. Students should be seated high enough to allow their forearms to rest easily on the desktop without pushing their shoulders upward.

Getting Started

Give your students a fresh start by beginning the day or a new activity with a short exercise or a series of them. This preparation helps students warm up so that you can bring the group into a single focus. You'll also find that these brain breaks help stave off the inevitable fidgeting, slouching, and wandering attentions that occur when children sit close together for long periods of time. You might choose one of these activities before starting calendar math, reading aloud, student presentations, or a mini-lesson.

Head to Toe

Start the day with this activity to awaken your class. Alternately, assign it individually to students who need to refocus. The slow, deep touch calms students while the quick, light touch awakens them.

When we're in good health, our ears and nose are a few degrees cooler than the rest of our bodies—just like dogs and cats!

Action

Count to six as you follow each step.

1. Rub your palms together fast. Feel the heat.

2. Rub your ears in circles. Squeeze your earlobes between your thumb and finger.

3. Rub the back of your head with your pointer fingers, moving toward your ears.

4. Rub big circles around your eyes with your fingertips, moving from your eyebrows to the top of your cheekbones and back up along the side of your nose.

5. Rub the sides of your nose using your pointer fingers.

6. Act like you're washing your whole face with your palms.

7. With your right hand, brush your left arm, from shoulder to fingertips, top and underside. Then switch sides.

8. Put one hand on top of the other on your stomach and make 6 circles.

9. Use both hands to rub your thighs.

10. Stomp your feet on the floor.

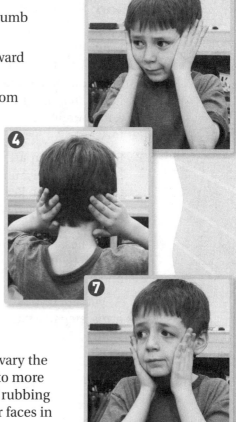

Expression

Since children respond to touch in different ways, you may want to vary the actions you name as students follow each step. Some may respond to more vigorous actions, such as gentle chopping on their thighs instead of rubbing in step 9. Others may prefer lightly tickling rather than rubbing their faces in steps 4–6.

Focus Ball

This simple exercise requires careful attention as students bend all of their 28 finger joints to form a the shape of a ball and then connect the movement of the focus ball with their breathing. The focused actions help students settle down and prepare for meeting time or a mini-lesson—a perfect opportunity for you to introduce new concepts, goals, and assignments.

Action: Part One

1. Stand with your feet and legs together.
2. Bring your fingertips together in front of your chest.
3. Bend all of your finger joints to form a ball shape with your hands.
4. Press your fingertips together firmly until you feel the muscles of your arms working. Can you feel the muscles all down the front of our body working, too?
5. See if you can hold that shape while you squeeze your legs together.

Action: Part Two

1. Press your hands and lower arms together, starting with your fingertips and ending with your elbows. Keep your hands in front of your chest and your fingers pointed forward.
2. Slowly "peel" apart your arms, in the same way: fingertips to elbows. Then keep going! Continue to reach your arms as far apart and away from your chest as they can reach. Extend them out to the sides and then behind you.
3. As you open your arms, step to a wide stance.

Variations

- Once students have created the ball with their hands, have them use it to mirror the action of their lungs and rib cage while breathing. Encourage them to use their hands like bellows and inhale as they inflate their focus ball and exhale as they press their palms and fingers flat together. It is challenging to coordinate the breath with movement and this will help build an ability to focus and concentrate on a task.

- A great brain break is to try an action in reverse. You can have students reverse the order of this exercise by beginning with Part Two, step 3 and ending with Part One, step 1.

- Repeat the action several times to improve circulation. Have students do Part One and Part Two as a full sequence three times.

Expression

Have students fill the imaginary ball between their hands with either a personal or group goal, like doing their best on a test, remembering to raise their hands before speaking, using words before taking action, or lining up quickly and quietly. Encourage them with the specific details and considerations that go into the chosen task. Then have them press their hands together, like compressing a digital file, or pressing a flower between a book, to save that intention.

Examples:

Thinking goals (e.g., in preparation for creative writing or lab work): *Imagine your mind as a home to a brilliant scientist, magician, or storyteller. Release this intention in front of your forehead.*

Feeling goals (e.g., in preparation for test taking or a presentation in front of peers): *Imagine yourself in the place where you feel the most relaxed and confident. Release this intention in front of your chest.*

Action goals (e.g., in preparation for leadership roles, or activities that require self control and individual responsibility): *Imagine yourself doing something you like to do that also helps other people. Release this intention in front of your power center, just below your navel.*

Hand-eye coordination supports the fine-motor skills necessary for drawing, writing, and handling manipulatives. To exercise hand-eye coordination and increase spatial awareness, ask students to focus on their hands using their peripheral, or side-to-side vision. They can practice this by holding their head and eyes steady on their hands in the "focus ball" position and keeping them focused on that spot as their hands move apart. Ask:

- *Can you see both hands all the time?*

- *How far to the side and back can you see?*

- *Do you notice when your vision changes from focusing front to focusing side to side?*

Standing Bow

In martial arts, bowing is a sign of mutual respect and self-control. Bowing low increases strength and flexibility in the torso and legs. It helps improve posture. Practicing bows can set the tone for the day.

Action: Master/Mistress Ichiban

1. Stand with your feet and legs together. Bend slowly at the hips and lean your head forward, gently pulling your shoulders back. You will make a 90-degree (right) angle between your back and your legs.

2. Stand up straight by lifting your head until you are upright.

Expression

Explain to the class that the simple bow (Mister/Mistress Ichiban), as well as the two kneeling bows that follow, the curtsy (Lady Seesafar), and the kneeling knight (Sir Knowsalot), are all part of ancient traditions. They show mutual respect among rulers, warriors, artists, craftsmen, great travelers, and wise women and men. Have students imagine that they are meeting a noble opponent as they perform a standing bow.

In my martial arts school, we spend some time every fall establishing protocol where children bow while using two hands to exchange objects with each other. It cuts down on the impulsive grabbing and tossing that can otherwise take place.

Kneeling Bow

In these versions of a bowing exercise, students must move gracefully. You might have students use these bows before and after they do partner or small-group work.

Action: Lady Seesafar

1. Stand with your feet and legs together. Cross your right leg behind your left leg. Bend both your knees.

2. Lower your body down and keep the ball of your right (back) foot on the floor. Bend until your right knee almost touches the floor.

3. Turn your head and nod slightly toward your left shoulder as if you're listening with your right ear.

4. Slowly return to standing. Repeat on the other side.

Action: Sir Knowsalot

1. Stand with your feet and legs together. Turn your palms in toward your sides.

2. Put your right hand over your heart.

3. Lower your chin, bend your knees, and slide your left leg straight behind you.

4. Continue to lower your body until both knees are bent at a 90-degree angle. Go down until your left knee touches the floor. (For an extra challenge, keep your knee an inch off the floor.)

5. Slowly return to standing. Repeat on the other side.

Expression

Tell students that they one day might be invited to visit the queen or the president! Have them picture paying a visit to a person who is famous for knowledge and power. Have them imagine that they are doing a kneeling bow at their meeting.

Brain Wave

This exercise gets the blood flowing and, at the same time, calms students who are overexcited. After this stretch, students will be ready to begin a lesson.

Action

1. Kneel on the floor. Put your feet down so that your toes are touching. Put your knees down, with a little distance between them.

2. Now rest your forearms and hands (palms down) on the floor. Spread your elbows wider than your knees.

3. Put your forehead on the floor between your hands.

4. Take a few deep breaths.

5. Push forward from your knees toward your head, rolling up until most of your weight is resting on your head and hands. Curve your back like the letter C.

6. Now move in reverse, shifting back to the resting kneel in step 2.

7. Repeat two times.

Safety Tip!

Use a mat, carpet square, rolled-up jacket, or soft notebook under students' heads if they are doing this exercise on a hard floor.

Expression

Read aloud the following to help students visualize and enhance the movement:

More than half your body is made up of water! Begin by feeling the water in your body swirling in small trickles and powerful waves within you. Make a wave inside yourself. Imagine one at the very bottom of your spine that swells to a crest between your shoulder blades. Then let it roll down into your head. Follow the wave back now, as it pushes from your head and reaches down your back. Imagine the undertow rushing back to the ocean. It is calm for a few seconds, and then a new wave begins to form.

X's and O's

This is a whole-body warm-up and core-strength builder. If students will be working independently, end the exercise on an "0." If you're starting whole-group or small-group work, then end on an "X."

Action

1. Sit on the edge of your chair. Make sure your feet are touching the floor.

2. Tuck in your arms, legs, and your whole body to make an "O" shape.

3. Spread your arms and legs wide open to create an "X" shape.

4. Curl back into the "O" position. Repeat.

Expression

Read aloud one or more of the following images to help students visualize the opening and closing actions.

* *You are a starfish. You're floating on a reef in the ocean. As you open and close your limbs, you feel the ebb and flow of the ocean.*

* *You are a morning glory blossom. You open to the sun in the morning, and after basking in the warmth, you close as the sun sets in the evening.*

* *You are a Venus flytrap. You snap closed to catch your lunch and hold tight as you digest the juicy fly. Then you open up again to wait for your next meal.*

Variations

* Repeat the exercise without letting students' feet touch the floor.

* Vary the tempo and add repetitions to make it more challenging.

* Ask students to notice all the places that bend on their body to make this exercise possible.

Tiger and Butterfly

This activity highlights the Four Brain-Break Essentials (see page 7), helping students practice grounding, self-space awareness, and self-control at a moderate or high energy level. Use this exercise as you prepare for whole-group or small-group work.

Action

1. Stand with your feet under your hips. Rise up on your tiptoes as you reach your arms up high above your head. Clasp your hands together as if catching something.

2. Slowly bend your ankles, knees, and hips to crouch down as low as you can. Bring your hands down in front of your face as if to peer inside.

3. Jump up to standing, releasing your hands.

4. Move your right arm and right leg across your body.

5. Open your right arm and leg wide apart to make a big "X."

6. Take a quick jump backward with your right leg.

7. Take two slow and gentle steps forward, reaching out in front of you.

Expression

Read aloud the following visualization:

You are a fierce tiger chasing a beautiful butterfly. It is fluttering above your head. Reach for it. You catch it [step 1] and pull it to down for a closer look. Your strong legs are crouching low [step 2]. The butterfly escapes! You jump up [step 3]. Where did it go? Is it behind the tall grass? Push the tall leaves aside with your big paws [steps 4 and 5]. A sharp sound startles you [make a loud clap] and you quickly take a step backward [step 6]. Be careful not to lose your balance! You finish your search with a few cautious steps forward. Reach for the butterfly if you see it appear in front of you [step 7].

The basis for this exercise is the Dimensional Scale, a movement exercise like a musical scale, created by movement theoretician Rudolf Laban (1879–1958).

Share the Air

This exercise is adapted from a series of warm-ups taught by Tai Chi Grandmaster Yu Cheng Hsiang. Use it to start the day, as a pick-me-up after lunch, or as a stretch to remedy lows in student energy.

Action

1. Try to complete these steps in one breath!

2. Stand with your feet hip-width apart and your arms at your sides.

3. Slowly inhale as you bend your elbows and lift your hands up, palms facing up until they are even with your chest.

4. Turn your hands outward and press with your palms into the space in front of you, reaching your arms forward.

5. Exhale as you lower your arms back down to your sides.

Expression

Lungs take up a lot of space, much more than children realize. Ask students to point to three places that mark the highest, deepest, and widest reaches of their lungs. You should get an interesting variety of responses! As they do the exercise, encourage them to sense that their lungs go as high as their shoulders, as wide as their outer ribcages, and as deep as their toes—this will help deepen their breathing and get plenty of oxygen to their brains.

Name Toss

This game helps students review and remember their classmates' names and makes a perfect group activity for beginning the year, welcoming new students, or boosting class spirits at any time. In addition to reviewing names in an enjoyable way, this name exercise develops students' cooperation, self-control, spatial awareness, and active-listening skills.

In advance, gather several easy-to-catch balls (diameters of about 8"–9" are easiest for children to catch). Arrange students in a circle (for more than 20 students, break into two circles). Start with one ball and when students are successful, add more balls to challenge the group. Students usually rise to the challenge and ask to use as many balls as possible. Have them work together to keep the balls in the air. You may want to assign one or two students to catch runaway balls.

Action

1. Go around the circle and have each student say his or her name. The group repeats each name. (Skip this step if everyone is familiar with one another.)

2. One player starts with the ball. This thrower looks at another person, says the person's name, and then throws the ball using a two-handed chest pass. The idea is to aim for a player's chest to make it easy to catch.

3. The catcher chooses a new person and follows step 2.

4. For older students, add in more balls, one at a time. By the end of the game, try to play with a ball for every three students.

> I always begin this game by reviewing the rules and letting students know that the success of the game depends on their ability to cooperate.

Expression

As each child speaks, he or she can choose to be expressive in saying, singing, or shouting the name. The group responds by echoing each name. Encourage students to use a similar rhythm, emphasis, and tone for each echo.

Variations

- Have students play while balancing on one leg.

- Begin by having students start in a low squat, stand to catch and throw, and then return to the squat position.

- Give each player three seconds to make the throw, counting to three out loud with the same speed and tone of voice for each student.

Management Tips!

Set a time limit prior to beginning a fun break like this one. Set an egg timer for five minutes and have everyone agree to stop when the timer sounds.

If the group is largely unfamiliar with one another, have everyone choose one person to throw the ball to before beginning the game. After a minute, stop the game and have everyone choose a new person.

Elasta-Kid

Use this stretch at the start of a lesson or after your class has been sitting for a long time. It teaches children to carve out a space for themselves while encouraging them to experiment with expanding and contracting their self-space. (See Four Brain-Break Essentials, page 7.)

Action

1. Keeping both feet on the ground, reach out your hands as far and wide as you can in all directions.

2. Lift your left leg. Stretch and reach your right arm under your leg. See how long you can keep that stretched-out feeling.

3. Come back to standing and try step 2 reaching your left arm under your right leg.

Expression

As they stretch, ask students to picture themselves moving through different materials, such as sticky cobwebs, melting wax, cold ice, hot glue, vegetable oil, dry leaves, and a car wash. Invite children to suggest their own images.

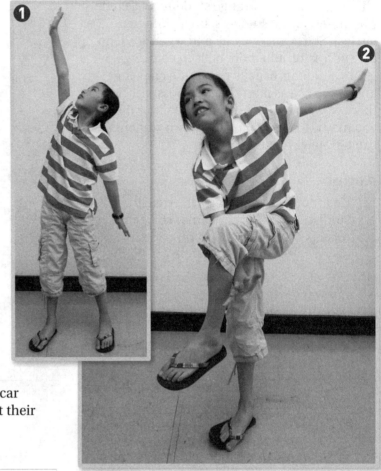

If students are moving in a small area, direct them to keep two feet on the ground at all times and bend down to reach each elbow to the opposite knee.

Refocusing

There are times when your students have endless energy. At other times, students have hit a low and need to recharge. During those times when students' energy level is interfering with their learning, try some of these refocusing brain breaks. Many of these exercises can be done while students are standing beside their desks. At other times, you might have some children stretch in a specially designated area of the classroom or in the hallway.

You can use these activities with the whole class or you can assign them to individual students who are in need of a break. Set a kitchen timer or give a finite number of repetitions so that you're not spending too much time away from academics.

Floating Heads

Try this exercise when your class has hit a low in energy or if you notice that many students are leaning on their desks or chairs. See Three Rules of Good Posture (page 8) for tips on helping them maintain a healthy, upright position.

Action

1. Stay where you are, either sitting or standing.

2. Move your head upward as if you could touch the ceiling.

Expression

Read aloud the following to help students visualize the action:

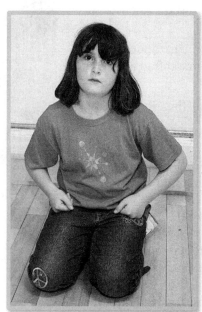
Before

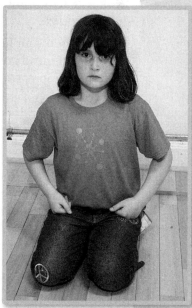
After

- *Imagine that your head is a balloon filled with helium. Let it rise to the ceiling, floating gently upward. Your spine is the string tied to the balloon, trailing behind. It is as light as a feather. Your legs are your anchor. Otherwise, you would float away.*

- *Your spine is like a radio antenna. It is ready to transmit and receive information. Pretend that you can set the dial for the kind of information that you would like to receive. Alert your senses to the signals nearby and far away. Imagine lifting up your spine and head so that your antenna can function better the higher it goes.*

The Sphinx

When students have trouble settling down to concentrate, try this stretch. It also makes a good follow-up exercise to Brain Wave (see page 13) and a good preparation for Equilateral, Isosceles, and Right Triangles (see pages 28–30).

Action

1. Kneel on the floor with your big toes touching and your knees close together, but not touching.

2. Put your hands and forearms on the floor with your elbows in front of your knees, fingers pointing straight ahead.

3. Rest your bottom on your heels.

4. Slide your body forward, leading with your forearms and hands and reaching and lifting your head as you go.

5. When your legs are extended, keep your head and torso lifted above your forearms.

6. Push back to kneeling. Repeat the exercise.

Expression

Have students imagine themselves as the mythical sphinx or as a resting house cat. To increase self-expression and help to relieve jaw tension, have children add exaggerated facial expressions. They can stick out their "cat" tongues and roll their eyes like lions. A more dynamic way to help students visualize steps 4 and 5 is to have them imagine themselves being shot out of a cannon at a circus or traveling down a tunnel.

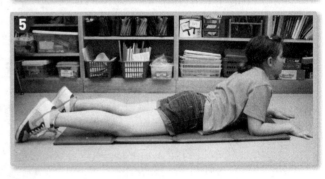

Make sure that students shift their weight from their shins and feet to slide forward or their forearms and hands to slide backward (see Variation).

Variation

Have students push backward into the sphinx position. Follow steps 1, 2, and 3. Then have them push back from their forearms and reach their head up and forward. At the same time, have them slide their legs straight out backwards.

Head Roll

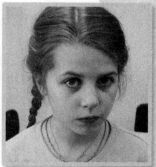

STEP 2: Eyes steady,
head moves side to side.

 Try this activity for a quick way to relax and refocus. It works well when combined with the Eye Roll (below).

Action

1. Hold your eyes steady on a spot directly in front of you. Nod your head up and down.

2. Hold your eyes steady on the spot while you turn your head from side to side.

3. Hold your eyes steady on the spot and tilt your head from side to side.

4. Roll your head slowly three times, first clockwise, then counterclockwise.

Expression

Have students act as if they are saying "Yes, teacher," for step 1, "No, teacher," for step 2, and "I don't know, teacher," for step 3.

Eye Roll

 This is another activity that offers fast relaxation and refocusing. Encourage students to go slowly and hold their heads still.

Action

1. Hold your head steady. Move your eyes from side to side.

2. Roll your eyes up and down.

3. Roll your eyes three times, first clockwise, then counterclockwise.

Expression

Your students may have heard adults tell them not to roll their eyes. Tell them that this kind of eye rolling is healthy and they should enjoy the permission to practice it!

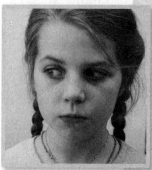

STEP 1: Head steady,
eyes move side to side.

Cross-Body Roll

Try this exercise when the class energy level is high, individual students are unfocused, or children need to wake up their whole bodies after a long period of sitting.

Action

1. Begin in the crab position, with your hands and feet on the floor and belly facing up.

2. Roll over to the left by swinging your right hand up and across your body. Twisting your upper body, place your hand on the floor next to your left hand.

3. Follow with your right leg. Let your leg roll you over until you are facing the floor.

4. Swing your left arm behind your head. Let your upper body and left leg follow until you end up back in the crab position.

5. Repeat the crossovers.

Expression

Students can think of themselves as blowing tumbleweeds or Tasmanian devils. After they have done the exercise once, have them brainstorm their own spiraling images.

Variations

- Have students cross over but stay in place. Use steps 1, 2, and 3 and then reverse directions, beginning to the left.

- Start the exercise crossing over with the legs, and have the arms follow.

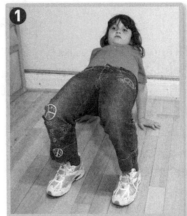

Have students follow their hands with their eyes to keep them focused and steady.

Skateboarding

 Get the blood circulating and give children a physical break if they're feeling squirmy. It helps students clear their heads to "take a ride" after sitting awhile.

Action

1. Stand with one hand on a wall or desk. Plant one foot on an imaginary skateboard. Slowly brush the floor with your other foot, starting with small movements.

2. Make movements larger and faster as you look over your right and left shoulders.

3. Switch sides and repeat.

Expression

Have students decide what kind of ride they're taking on their skateboards. It can be a leisurely ride home or a race against another skateboarder. Ask children to picture and describe what they see. Are there curbs to jump or hills to climb? Do they crouch down as they pass the window of a cranky neighbor?

Variations

Students may enjoy experimenting with these skateboarding tricks, which can improve balance and core strength.

- To "shoot the curb," students can add a single leg hop after brushing their foot four times.

- To "coast," have students put their weight on one leg while holding the other leg straight out, off the floor in front.

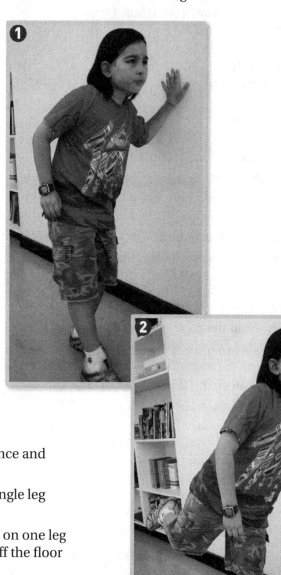

Pitch Perfect

This exercise requires good balance, timing, control, and spatial awareness. You can play with the whole class, with each child beside a desk and you as the umpire. Students can also play individually apart from the group. To control the amount of time spent on the mound, assign a set number of pitches.

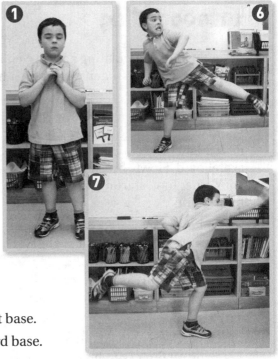

Action

1. Take a pitcher's stance. Hold an imaginary ball in front of your chest.

2. Pick a pitch and adjust your grip as you need to. Decide if you'll throw a fastball, a curve, a slider, or a knuckleball.

3. Look over your left (or right) shoulder to first base.

4. Look over your right (or left) shoulder to third base.

5. Look straight ahead and nod twice.

6. Wind up and throw the ball.

7. Hold the position at end of the pitch for a count of 5.

8. Return to your position on the mound.

Have students follow their hands with their eyes to keep them focused and steady.

Expression

If you choose to be umpire, use the following images to guide your students and keep the exercise organized. Have students visualize the catcher, look for the strike zone between the batter's shoulders and knees, and hear the spectators as they alternate between hushed anticipation and resounding cheers. Remind students to keep their eye on the ball!

Windmills

This exercise utilizes all of the developmental patterns (see page 5). It is a whole-body stretch for refocusing, resetting, and giving children a challenge.

Action

1. Stand with your feet hip-width apart. Raise your arms over your head, palms facing forward.

2. Circle your left arm in front as your right arm circles back.

3. Repeat five times in this direction.

4. Reverse directions and repeat five more times.

Expression

Read aloud the following: *Feel the energy that you create with your windmill. Do the exercise as fast as you can for 20 seconds. Stop. Can you feel the blood pulsing in your fingers? Think about it—you moved it there with the force you created using your arms as a windmill!*

Variations

- Once students have mastered the windmill exercise, have them create a waterwheel, by adding in leg motions. As they move their right arm forward, they raise their right knee and slap it with their left hand (see photo at right).

- Once the waterwheel is mastered, have students add a piston action. They should hop on one leg at the same time that they slap their lifted knee.

Karate Kicks

Aerobic exercise stimulates the brain to produce hormones that increase cognitive performance. At the same time, an active exercise like this one can help children burn off the excess energy that can interfere with schoolwork.

Action

1. Stand with your hands on your hips and feet under your hips.

2. Kick your right leg high in front of you. (A solid kick includes three parts: first, draw your knee up, then extend your leg straight out in front of you, and last, draw your knee back in.)

3. Kick your right leg up high.

4. Repeat, alternating right and left.

STEP 2: Three-part kick

Expression

Have students take turns counting sets of 10 or 20, being careful to count and then kick (e.g., *One*, [kick], *two*, [kick], . . .) Moving to the count helps children practice self-control and it also helps the whole group kick together, which can be quite powerful.

Variations

- To increase balance and control, have students hold out the opposite hand, with their palm facing down at about their waist, as a target for their kicks. They will use their left hand as they lift their right knee and vice versa.

- For a different challenge or when space is limited, substitute a knee kick, maintaining a bent-leg position in step 2.

On the Run

Try this to start the day or as a quick break between lessons. This is another form of aerobic exercise that can support cognitive performance while simultaneously channeling students' extra energy.

Action

1. Begin by walking in place for 30 seconds.

2. Increase your speed. Jog in place for 30 seconds.

3. Go even faster. Sprint in place for 15 seconds. Then jog in place for 45 seconds.

4. Repeat.

Expression

- Choose a student to lead a call-and-response session. The leader can begin a military-style chant, such as, "One, two!" to which the group responds, "Three, four!" With the same format, they can recite math facts!

- Help students visualize a favorite place to imagine running. Describe a beach, a rain forest, or a park that they're running through—or project a nature scene onscreen.

Tell students that it will take them about 10 to 12 minutes to run a mile. They'll feel very proud to accomplish this!

Variation

For an extra challenge, have students run in place, first raising their knees to their waists for 15 seconds. For the next 15 seconds, have them kick back to their bottoms. Alternate these two actions for several rounds.

Transitioning

A smooth transition is priceless. A rough transition wastes time, drains physical and mental energy, and wears down your patience. These exercises are meant to help make lesson-to-lesson and room-to-room transitions smooth. Use them before you have students line up or while you are handing out supplies for the next lesson. For some of these brain breaks, children sit on the floor. Sitting well promotes good circulation and allows more oxygen to get to the brain. Offer your students a variety of sitting choices to provide small transitions during a long group meeting or mini-lesson. They will feel refreshed with each change. Point out that a change is as good as a rest!

With these kinds of exercises, you can help students recover from lagging muscles and minds. You might also offer brain breaks like these as a positive reinforcement. Invite students to do them in exchange for schoolwork completed or when small groups have done well.

Iron Caterpillar

Between lessons, incorporate this exercise as a break. If there is room, you can also have students do it beside their desks as a means of redirecting excess energy.

Action

1. Put your hands on the floor in front of your feet.

2. Leave your feet where they are and walk your hands forward until your body is parallel to the floor. End up so you're in a push-up position.

3. Now leave your hands where they are and walk your feet up to your hands.

4. Repeat, going forward and back. Alternate moving your hands and your feet.

5. Stand up slowly.

Expression

Read aloud as students bend: *Fold yourself in half. Now flatten yourself out!*

At the end of the exercise, make sure that children stand up slowly to avoid a head rush.

Equilateral Triangle

Encourage balanced thinking by having students sit in a position that promotes physical and mental equilibrium. The Equilateral Triangle helps children consider two solutions to a problem—they can weigh one solution as they gesture with the left hand and another solution as they gesture with the right.

Action

1. Sit cross-legged on the floor.
2. Rest each of your arms on your legs. Open your hands, palms facing up.

Expression

Have students picture themselves as a scale. Tell them to hold out their hands as if they are weighing and balancing two things. Explain that this is the preferred sitting posture of wise men and women.

"Balanced" expression

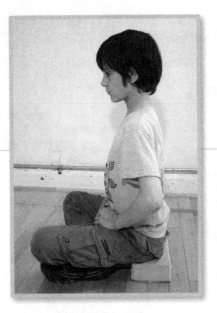

A child who lacks core strength or hip flexibility will find it difficult to maintain the natural curves of the spine (page 8). The child may slouch forward with rounded shoulders and lower back in an exaggerated C-curve. Offer a remedy by having the child use a prop such as a yoga block, a rolled blanket or pillow, or even a soft book to sit on. This elevates and positions the pelvis to better support the spine.

Isosceles Triangle

This position enables children to sit taller. The change in self-perception encourages them to participate more actively, listen more receptively, and pay closer attention. As it provides more spinal support than the Equilateral Triangle posture, students may find it more comfortable. Plus, it strengthens their legs!

Action

1. Sit on the floor.
2. Fold your legs underneath you so that your heels make a seat for your bottom.
3. Lay the tops of your feet and toes flat on the floor.

Expression

Tell students that this is the favored position of the samurai, elephant riders, and acrobats.

Variation

For a challenge and an energy-boosting break, have students jump from this position to standing, without using their hands.

> **C**hildren whose ankles are inflexible will have difficulty in this position, so they should switch to the Equilateral or Right Triangle posture after a short while. A rolled towel under the student's ankles can provide support until the child has developed greater flexibility.

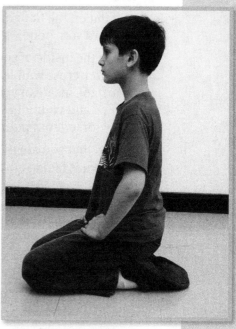

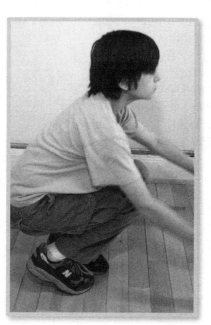

Variation

Right Triangle

When students use this sitting posture, make sure that they spend time on both sides. If children spend too much time sitting on one side, their muscle tone will be imbalanced. Show students that they can easily stand up from this position by spiraling upward.

Action

1. Sit flat on the floor and draw your heels toward you, bending your knees.

2. Turn the inside of your right leg to face up and cross your leg in front of you. Turn the inside of your left leg to face down and your fold your leg beside you, so your left foot points behind you.

3. Sit so that you are mostly resting on the leg that is facing up.

4. Switch sides. This time, turn your left leg so it crosses in front, thigh facing up, and fold back your right leg, thigh facing down.

Expression

Tell students that this is the favored position of queens on horseback.

Variation

You can designate one student as timekeeper and have all the students hold their positions for a set amount of time. You may have children sit for as long as 5 minutes at a time in any one posture, but begin by setting the timer for short intervals and then, as students get accustomed to the position, gradually lengthen the intervals.

Encourage children who sit in a W shape, with their knees facing inward and legs folded back, flat on the floor (shown at right), to sit in a more supportive triangle position (shown above).

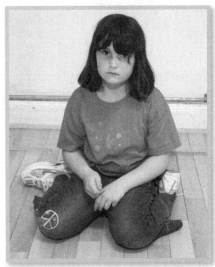

Help students find an alternative for the unsupportive "W" position.

Rolling Triangles

Once children are familiar with the different sitting triangles (Equilateral, Isosceles, and Right, pages 28–30), incorporate each of them into this moderate-energy exercise. Try this before beginning a group lesson or when students are fidgeting and need a break.

Action

1. Sit in the Isosceles Triangle position.
2. Lean sideways onto your right hip until you end up in a Right Triangle.
3. Turn your left leg over to change to an Equilateral Triangle posture.
4. Turn your right leg over to make the Right Triangle.
5. Shift your hips forward to go back to the Isosceles Triangle.
6. Repeat, starting to the left.

Expression

Ask students to imagine that the great pyramids are rolling along the desert floor as though blown sideways by the wind. Have students stay stable and then mobilize! Also have them notice triangles in their world. How many triangles can students see around them? How many triangles can they make with their bodies? Have them notice triangles between their elbows and knees and between their necks and shoulders.

Variations

- For more stability work, have students try this sequence while holding their arms in the air or their hands on their heads or shoulders.
- Call out triangle position names in a random order. Have students move into them, without using their hands for support.
- Have students move from triangle sitting to standing and back, without using their hands.

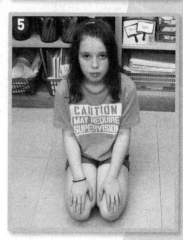

Most children will need to use their hands to propel them through some part of the exercise. Allow them to do this, but encourage them to rely on their hips and knees and core muscles. When they do this exercise regularly, over time they will become stronger and more flexible and will no longer need to use their hands for support.

Bucking Bronco

A strong torso is essential for a healthy sitting posture and effortless writing. This exercise helps children build upper body strength and get their fidgets out so they can reengage in learning. Students will love it!

Action

1. Begin with your hands and knees on the floor, hands under your shoulders and knees under your hips like a table.

2. Put all of your weight on your hands and kick your feet high in the air. Let your feet drop back to the floor.

3. Then put all of your weight on your knees and clap your hands.

4. Repeat 20 times.

Expression

Read aloud the following to help students visualize the action: *You are a wild horse. Someone is trying to ride on your back, and you don't like it! Can you buck the rider off? Try bucking fast! Now try kicking slowly. Can you hold a kick in the air?*

Variation

Have students try combinations of claps and kicks, such as three claps followed by two kicks.

If children find it hard to get their kicks off the ground, give them a visual target. Direct their attention to your hand, which you should hold behind them, just outside of their kicking reach.

Smart Feet Sitting

Help students see that caring for their feet helps them prepare for learning. Droidge writes that when feet are challenged by a variety of surfaces, there is greater sensory feedback to the brain—in fact, the soles of our feet contain thousands of nerve endings just waiting to communicate information!

If it is practical in your classroom, have children remove their shoes and wiggle their toes, massage their arches and perform this exercise while standing. End the standing version by having students bounce once or twice to benefit the immune system.

Action

Do each step to a count of 10.

1. With your shoes off, sit cross-legged in an Equilateral Triangle (page 28).

2. Stretch your right leg out, along the floor.

3. Hold your left foot. With your thumb, touch the inside of your heel, just below your ankle. Massage it in circles.

4. Massage along the inside of the arch of your foot and your big toe.

5. Hold your left ankle with both hands and shake your foot hard.

6. Repeat with your right foot.

Expression

Explain to students that their feet can do most things that their hands can do. You might even challenge them to try to pick up a pencil or clap with their feet. Read: *Did you know that your feet have fifty-two bones? That's one-fourth the total number of bones in the body!*

Smart Feet Standing

This exercise directs children to pay close attention to their feet, which requires a shift in thinking and concentration. Use it to give students a calm break between lessons.

Action

Do each step to a count of 10.

1. Stand with your feet hip-width apart.

2. Wiggle your toes by pressing them into the floor, one by one, big toe to little toe.

3. Wriggle your toes by lifting them off the floor, one by one, big toe to little toe.

4. Spread your toes apart then squish them together.

5. Move your big toes toward each other.

6. Roll to the outside edges of your feet.

7. Roll to the inside edges of your feet.

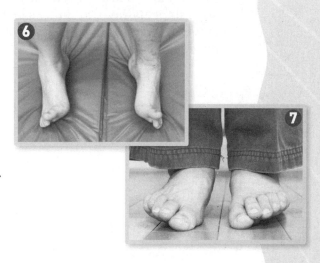

8. Lift your body up onto your tiptoes.

9. Lower yourself back down to your heels.

10. Repeat steps 8 and 9 faster and faster.

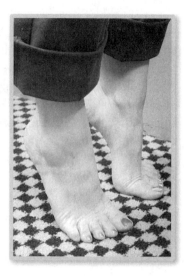

Expression

Read aloud the following to help students visualize the action:

Imagine that you're standing in a squishy mud puddle or on the wet sand at the beach. Feel the mud or sand squish up through your toes. The longer you stand there, the deeper your feet sink down. Feel the mud or sand slide off the top of your feet as you roll to the inside and outside. Rise out of the muck to balance on your tiptoes. At last, your whole body is jiggling up and down. Coins are falling from your pockets as you bounce.

Wriggling

 Thirty seconds spent doing this exercise will bring circulation, vitality, and awareness back to the spine. Try this after a long test or when students seem sleepy at their desks.

Action

1. Begin with your hands and knees on the floor, hands under your shoulders and knees under your hips, like a table.

2. Wriggle, roll, and twist your back in different ways while you count to 20.

Expression

Have students imagine that their backs are like a roller coaster track with steep hills, valleys, and sharp corners. Have them arch their backs to make a big hill, reverse it to form a deep valley, flatten it out for a straightaway, and slither sideways for curves. Vary the speed to help them practice self-control.

Chair Push-Ups

 This exercise will help children who have energy to burn! The steps are arranged in increasing order of difficulty. Have students do them individually or as a series.

Action: Part One

1. As you sit in a chair, grasp the front of your seat, curling your fingers under to grip the edge.
2. With your feet flat on the floor and your knees bent, slide your body off your chair. Hold yourself up with your arms.
3. Bend your elbows and lower your body in front of the chair.
4. Straighten your elbows and raise your body back up.
5. Repeat 5 to 25 times.

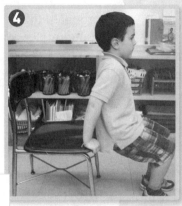

Part One

As a challenge, have children keep their elbows close to their body during Part One.

Action: Part Two

1. Place a hand on each side of your chair seat.
2. Straighten and raise both legs in the air.
3. Bend and lower your legs.
4. Repeat 10 to 20 times.

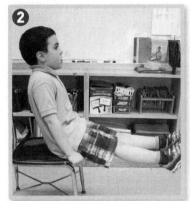

Part Two

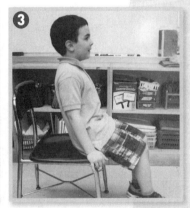

Action: Part Three

1. Place a hand on each side of your chair seat.
2. Push down on your hands and tilt your body forward a little bit.
3. Lift yourself up off the chair.
4. Lower yourself back down.
5. Repeat 10 to 20 times.

Expression

Encourage students to enjoy the physical challenge of this exercise, especially the satisfaction of completing it! Ask students if they notice a change in their muscles, their breathing, or the temperature of their bodies.

Variation

Students can keep a journal, tracking their progress to see how many of each part they can do. Alternately, select a student to monitor the progress of the whole class. You might offer coaching jobs like this one on a rotating basis.

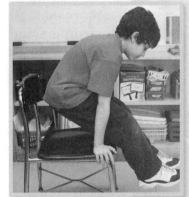

Part Three

Calming and Concentrating

At times when students are required to sit still and think deeply for long periods, you want to help them achieve a sense of calm and focus. For instance, you may be introducing a new unit or reviewing one and you want to be sure that students are prepared to listen attentively. And when students are doing independent writing or taking standardized assessments, their concentration level should be at its highest.

The following exercises help students attain a mind-body balance that will serve them well as they focus on learning. As students stretch and breathe, be sure to share imagery that will help them clear their minds.

Shake It Off

Try this exercise after students have been sitting in front of the computer or working for a long time at their desks. It quickly restores circulation and vitality to the spine. Students feel refreshed and are ready to concentrate.

Action

1. Stand facing your desk, at least a foot away from it, with your arms at your sides.

2. Grasp the edge of your desk, with your palms down.

3. Keep your hands and feet in place as you move your spine in a rolling motion from top to bottom. Move your spine in a zigzag motion from side to side, and then move your spine in a twisting motion.

4. Mix all three motions. Repeat.

Expression

Suggest that students shake themselves like a dog that has just come from the bath or a swim. Tell them to make sure they shake the water off of their heads and their tails!

Encourage a variety of movement, knowing that for some children, this will mean more movement and for others it will mean less.

Breathe In, Breathe Out

This easy exercise will help your class focus and find their balance. You can use it when children need to calm down or you need to quickly transition them. Have students try to match your breathing pace as you quickly inhale and then slowly exhale.

Action

1. Raise your arms to chest level. Breathe in deeply through your nose. Pull your hands toward your chest, palms facing up.

2. Breathe out as slowly as you can through your mouth. Slowly push your hands down the front of your body until all the air has gone out.

3. Repeat two times.

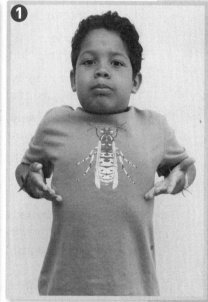

Expression

As students focus on breathing, have them imagine that they are waking up in a beautiful place, such as the top of a mountain, a cliff overlooking the sea, or a dense forest.

When we inhale, the brain releases stimulating alpha neurons. When we exhale, calming beta neurons are released. By doing both, we strike the balance between relaxed and alert states.

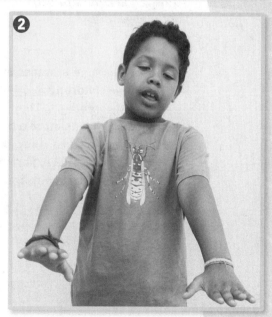

Belly Breathing

 Focus on belly breathing to help students remain calm during times that they find stressful, such as class presentations or test taking.

Action

1. Put both hands on your belly.
2. Close your eyes. Think only about your breathing. Concentrate!
3. Feel your belly move toward your hands as you take a breath in, or inhale.
4. Feel your belly move away from your hands as you breathe out, or exhale.
5. Repeat three times.

Expression

Have students imagine a long straw with a balloon attached at the bottom. The straw begins at their nose and ends just below their belly button. Read aloud:

Every time you breathe into your straw, the air travels down the straw to fill the balloon. Feel the balloon get full.

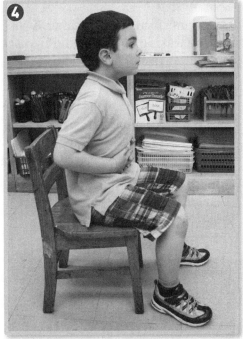

Not everyone breathes in the same way. Some children are chest breathers rather than belly breathers. They may find that their bellies and hands move a little differently as they inhale and as they exhale. Recognize students' individual experiences, while exposing them to beneficial belly breaths.

3-D Breathing

This exercise is an excellent way to raise students' spatial awareness and improve their self-control. Emphasize inhaling when you want to wake the class up and exhaling when you want to calm them down.

Action

1. Stand with your feet and legs together. Inhale as you reach your arms out wide to both sides and then up above your head. Keep stretching until your palms touch over your head.

2. Exhale as you lower your hands. Keep your palms together and gently drop them straight down until they reach your belly button.

3. Inhale as you point your hands straight ahead. Keep your palms together and stretch your arms out in front of your body.

4. Exhale as you rotate your arms. Turn your palms outward and spread your arms to the side as if you are swimming breaststroke.

5. Inhale as you return your arms to your sides.

6. Exhale as you stand still.

7. Repeat twice.

Expression

Have students notice what happens to the shape of their bodies when they inhale and exhale.

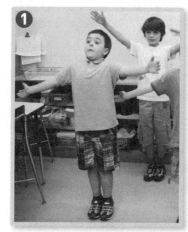

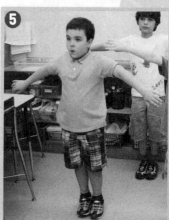

Invisible Kids

Try this exercise to engage students in the challenge of holding steady. Use it when you need to have students remain quietly in one place for a long stretch or anytime you want the whole class paying attention to you!

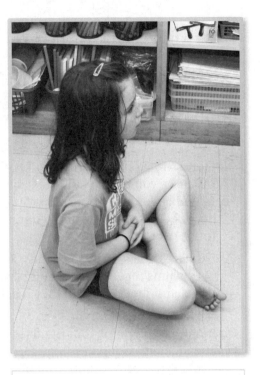

Action

1. Choose a good standing or seated position.

2. Be as still and quiet as possible, noticing the sights, sounds, and smells around you. Keep breathing and noticing how your body feels.

Expression

- While students are holding still, encourage them to pay attention to their bodies. Read aloud the following: *Notice your heart beating. Feel your eyelids blinking. Feel your breath moving through your ribcage, your belly, and your back. Hold your eyes steady. How much of the room can you still see without moving your eyes? Listen. Think about what you can hear.*

> **S**low and even breathing through the nose will enhance this exercise. Doing a longer exhale promotes relaxation and focus.

- Tell students that although legends say that ninja had the ability to disappear, this is likely an exaggeration of their highly developed stealth and stillness skills, which they learned from the animal kingdom. Read aloud the following: *Imagine yourself as a ninja. Pretend that you are invisible. Feel the spell that you create through your absolute stillness. You've got the power of ninja (or Dumbledore, Merlin, or Gandalf).*

- Have students choose to be an animal that keeps still, such as a chameleon, snow rabbit, or stick bug.

Variations

- Have students move from one place to another, imagining that they are silently blending in the whole time.

- Set a timer. Have students count the noises they can hear. Have a contest to see who can take the fewest breaths before the timer goes off.

- Play Surprise Attack. Designate a set of sound warnings. When students hear the warning, they become invisible until the signal comes to release the spell. You can use a red light and green light signal or a bell, for example.

- Have children imagine themselves growing and shrinking beyond their body's walls. Students who enjoy performing and have stage presence will be motivated to work on this.

Fuzz Busters

This warm-up invigorates students as they begin their day. It also serves as a good recuperation from long periods sitting still and enables them to concentrate afterward.

Fuzz! If we stay put for too long, it takes over like rust on a wintering bike. Movement melts it away!

Action

1. Stand, feet hip-width apart. Raise your arms up over your head. Reach for the ceiling.

2. Keep reaching as you lean to the right. Reach for the wall or window.

3. Reach over to the left as far as you can.

4. Come back to the center. Stand up straight and lower your arms.

5. Nod your head forward. Roll down your spine bit by bit. Let your arms hang down until your hands touch the floor. Hold for a count of ten.

6. Gently roll your body back up to standing.

Expression

Read aloud the following: *The fuzz is melting away like cotton candy on your tongue or a snake shedding its skin. Move smoothly, like an eel slipping through the water. Can you go so slowly that you can feel the fuzz melting? Now move faster. Can you zip away the fuzz in an instant?*

Swinging Samurai

When students are restless or having trouble concentrating on a task, offer this exercise. You may want to designate an area of the classroom for individual students to use for this activity. If you work in a group, form a circle. Have each child swing inward toward a central target.

Action

1. Stand, feet hip-width apart. Raise both hands above your head as if you are holding a sword.

2. Keep your eyes steady on a target straight ahead as you lunge forward on your right leg. Bring your arms down to cut through your imaginary target.

3. Without letting your knee touch the floor, hold this position for a count of ten.

4. Return to standing. Repeat on the other side.

Expression

Help students envision different materials they are slicing through, such as wood, butter, water, or steel. Discuss how this changes the movement.

Variations

- Have students lunge backwards as they cut.

- Change the tempo so that students are swinging quickly and slowly.

- To improve balance and coordination, have students hold one arm behind their back and swing their imaginary sword with the other. Repeat on the other side.

Push-Ups

 Give your students some push-ups to do when they have finished work early, when they are late to class, or anytime they are fidgety. Children love them!

Action

1. Squat down and walk your hands forward into a plank position. Your body should be parallel to the floor.

2. Bend your elbows and lower your body to almost touch the floor. Keep your body flat.

3. Push up. Repeat five to ten times.

Expression

Have students imagine that they are pushing the floor away from them instead of pushing themselves away from the floor. Tell the class to all work together to push the floor away. Have them imagine that they are pushing away heavy objects, such as boulders, or even the Empire State Building.

Variations

- Allow children who struggle with standard push-ups to do modified push-ups. They can push off a wall or a chair. They can also rest their knees on the floor as they push with their elbows.

- Have children hold each push-up low to the floor for a count of five.

- Hold the lifted push-up position for 10 to 30 seconds.

Variation

Walking the Halls

If your class isn't settled as they move through the school building, you probably find that your stress level escalates as students' ability to control their volume and fidgeting decreases. Help prepare students for walking the halls by giving them exercises to practice before and during their travels. The imagery you provide will help students stay calm and enjoy their walks—and help you efficiently transport the class.

These traveling breaks are fun ways for children to practice self-control, self-space awareness, and good grounding skills while moving as a group through the school. Once you've introduced them, your class will look forward to doing them again and again.

Seeds and Sculptures

The simple act of changing levels from standing to squatting low is excellent exercise for everyone. It will increase overall circulation, grounding, and self-space awareness. Changing tempos will help students regulate their movement and exercise self-control in preparation for a walk through the halls.

Action

1. Begin in a squatting position with your heels on the ground.

2. Try to keep your heels to the ground as you slowly stand up.

3. Once you are standing, reach your arms above your head.

4. Melt back down to your original position.

5. Repeat three times.

Expression

* Begin this exercise by asking students what seeds need in order to grow, and use their answers to fuel the exercise. Seeds need room to grow. (Make sure that there is room for students to expand and reach all around themselves.) Seeds need strong roots that keep them from blowing away, and lots of rain. (As a signal to start growing, you may want to go around and gently sprinkle imaginary rain on their heads and backs with gentle tapping.) Once students are standing up, they can sway to the breezes and lift their faces toward the sun. Fall will come, causing the flowers to wither and sink to the ground.

- Use an image of an ice sculpture with students starting out as a block of ice, frozen and compact. As the sculptor goes to work, a shape, such as an animal, an athlete, a letter of the alphabet, slowly emerges. Once the shape is fully realized, it begins to melt under the hot sun.

Variation

This is a good exercise to introduce a competitive element. Ask students, *How slow can you go? How smooth and evenly paced can you keep the movement?*

Stealth Walk

This exercise, adapted from a meditation ritual, works well when students are lining up and moving from room to room. It reinforces a sense of self-space and helps students make transitions cooperatively.

Action

1. Line up in single file. You should stand an arm's length behind the person in front of you.

2. Look at the feet of the person in front of you. (Just turn your eyes downward, not your whole head.)

3. Begin with the right foot and take a step. Keep stepping at the same time and speed as the person in front of you.

Expression

- To help students sharpen their focus, challenge them to imagine walking on a tightrope, a rope bridge over a canyon, or a perilous pathway on the side of a mountain peak.

- Point out that when everyone is stepping together, only one set of footsteps can be heard! Sneaking from place to place will increase everyone's focus and slow the pace.

Add a check-point with a "freeze" signal. At this time, students stop to check their distance.

Variations

- Add a timing component by clapping or singing songs in unison. Students can do a line chant of "Left! Right!" or a simple song such as, "Hi-ho, hi-ho, it's off to class we go."
- Have students use only peripheral vision to notice details around them.

Duck Walk

Try this exercise when your class has excess energy or alternately, when students need to wake up their legs after long periods of sitting. They will arrive at their destination ready to focus!

Action

1. Squat down on your heels.
2. Tuck in your arms to make wings.
3. Duck walk to your destination.

Expression

- Tell students that they are ducklings. From time to time, have them stretch their necks or shake out their feathers. When they arrive, they can shake each of their webbed feet.
- Older students might enjoy knowing that this is a traditional exercise of the Shaolin monks, who walk and climb stairs in this position to develop legs of steel.

Variations

- Have students change levels, rising and sinking more dramatically with each step. This will slow them down.
- To improve their balance, challenge children to keep their hands behind their back as they duck walk.

Some students will find this very demanding due to tight ankles, hamstrings, and lower back muscles. It should be fun! If children are having too much trouble, they don't have to bend as low in their squats.

If there is a designated line leader in your class, you might also assign a special line closer. The closer makes sure that nothing has been left behind, the lights are off, and the doors and windows are closed. As the line proceeds, the closer checks that the line maintains a good formation from tip to tail throughout the transition.

Crab Walk

 Save this exercise for those days when your class needs an extra boost! It will raise spirits and, at the same time, utilize excess energy, build whole-body strength, and improve coordination. Finish this activity with Breathe In, Breathe Out (see page 37) for a well-rounded break.

Action

1. Put your hands and your feet on the floor, with your belly up.

2. Crab walk to your destination. You may move in any direction.

Expression

Have children picture themselves as a group of crabs traveling across a rocky seashore. They are helping each other get from one rock to the next!

Bear Walk

The Bear Walk and Elephant Walk can be combined with the follow-the-leader concepts of Stealth Walk (see page 45). Students stay aware of their classmates as they move from room to room.

Action

1. Put your hands and feet on the floor, facing down.

2. Walk forward by moving your right hand and right foot at the same time. Then move your left hand and left foot at the same time.

3. Keep walking with this pattern. If you're in a line, follow the person in front of you.

Expression

Have students think of themselves as bears on a hunt, walking quietly through the forest. Tell them that when they see their prey, they should quicken their pace.

Variation

Combine Bear Walk and Elephant Walk (page 48). Give a cue to switch between the two walks to help children stay focused on what they are doing.

Elephant Walk

 Try this as a creative way to have children prepare for lining up. It is another means to remind students to maintain their self-space.

Action

1. Put your hands and feet on the floor, facing down.

2. Walk forward by moving your right hand and left foot at the same time. Then move your left hand and your right foot together.

3. Keep walking with this pattern. If you're in a line, follow the person in front of you.

Expression

Elephants are the largest animals on land and have no natural predators within the animal kingdom. They are known for their intelligence and excellent memory. While students can feel fearless as they walk as elephants, their steps should reflect their large size, heavy weight, and thoughtfulness.

Variations

- Vary the tempo: moving slowly will improve balance and core strength; moving quickly will vigorously exercise the arms and legs and require more focus for the group to stay together.

- If your destination is far enough away, switch between Elephant Walk and Bear Walk (page 47).

Brain

Wriggling

Try this after a long test or when you are feeling sleepy at your desk.

1 Begin with your hands and knees on the floor.

2 Wriggle, roll, and twist your back in different ways while you count to 20.

Brea
Brea

**This easy
you calm c**

Breaks

Elasta-Kid

Try this stretch as a warm-up for reading, writing, and raising your hand!

1 Keeping both feet on the ground, reach out your hands as far and wide as you can in all directions.

2 Stretch and reach your right arm through your left leg. Then stretch your left arm through your right leg. See how long you can keep that stretched-out feeling.

athe In,
the Out

exercise is sure to help
Iown and focus.

1 Raise your arms to

Bucking Bronco

Get your fidgets out so you can get down to business!

1. Begin with your hands and knees on the floor.

2. Put all of your weight on your hands and kick your feet high in the air.

3. Then put all of your weight on your knees and clap your hands.

4. Repeat 20 times.

chest level. Breathe in deeply through your nose. Pull your hands toward your chest, palms facing up.

2 Breathe out as slowly as you can through your mouth. Slowly push your hands down the front of your body until all the air is out.

3 Repeat two times.

Skateboarding

Need to clear your head? Go for a ride!

1 Stand with one hand on a wall or desk. Plant one foot on an imaginary skateboard. Slowly brush the floor with your other foot, starting with small movements.

2 Make the movements larger and faster as you look over your right and left shoulder.

3 Switch sides and repeat.